Charlie New Book 2025

The Book of Sheen From Wall Street to Winning

Copyright © 2025

All rights reserved. No part of this publication may be reproduced, distributed, or transmitted in any form or by any means, including photocopying, recording, or other electronic or mechanical methods, without the prior written permission of the publisher, except in the case of brief quotations embodied in critical reviews and certain other noncommercial uses permitted by copyright law.

Table of contents

Table of contents 3
Chapter 1 4
Born Into Spotlight 4
Chapter 2 8
The Dreamer and the Rebel 8
Chapter 3 12
Breaking Through: Hollywood Calling 12
Chapter 4 16
Fame at Full Speed 16
Chapter 5 20
The Shadow of Addiction 20
Chapter 6 24
Love, Lust, and Loss 24
    Chapter 7 28
    Sitcom King: Winning at Prime Time 28
    Chapter 8 32
    Meltdown in the Spotlight 32
    Chapter 9 35
    Fallout and Reinvention 35
    Chapter 10 38
    Facing the Truth 38
    Chapter 11 41
    Redemption and Recovery 41
    Chapter 12 44
    Legacy of Laughter and Chaos 44
    Chapter 13 47
    A New Chapter: Life After the Headlines .. 47

Chapter 1

Born Into Spotlight

I was born with a last name that carried more weight than I could possibly understand at the time. For most kids, childhood is about scraped knees, after-school games, and dreams that stretch no further than the next summer vacation. For me, childhood came with boom mics, movie sets, and the kind of attention that said, *this kid belongs to somebody important.*

My father, Martin Sheen, was already a rising actor by the time I came into the world. To the rest of the world, he was a face they recognized from the big screen, the man who would one day be known for *Apocalypse Now* and a career that seemed untouchable. To me, he was Dad—the guy who carried himself with equal parts humility and fire, who treated every role as if it were his last, and who somehow still found the time to coach me and my brothers on how to throw a baseball in the backyard.

Growing up in Malibu, I lived in a world that many people could only imagine. The ocean was our backdrop, the neighborhood kids were often children of directors, musicians, or producers, and the idea of Hollywood wasn't a dream to chase—it was a living, breathing part of everyday life. Fame wasn't something I admired from afar. Fame lived next door, drove past our house, and sometimes sat across the dinner table.

But here's the truth: when you're a kid, you don't know what fame really is. You don't understand the machine, the pressure, the way the spotlight can either warm you or burn you alive. All I knew was that my dad had a job that people talked about, and that sometimes, when he walked into a room, the air seemed to change.

What I did know was that I wanted to follow in his footsteps—not because I was chasing the glow of fame, but because I was mesmerized by the way stories could live on through film. I remember being on set, watching cameras roll, lights shift, and people whisper about the "magic of the scene." To a boy like me, it felt like stepping into another universe.

But being a Sheen wasn't just about opportunity. It was also about expectation. From teachers to neighbors, everyone seemed to know who my father was, and by extension, who I was supposed to be. That's the kind of pressure you don't notice at first—it creeps in. You start to ask yourself: *Am I living my life, or am I playing out a role I was born into?*

My early brushes with fame came quietly at first—small roles, auditions, introductions to people who could open doors. But long before Hollywood really called my name, I was just a kid navigating two worlds: the ordinary, where I wanted to play baseball and sneak comic books under the covers, and the extraordinary, where my last name made people watch me a little too closely.

Looking back now, I realize how much those years shaped me. Malibu gave me sunshine, freedom, and the illusion that life could always be golden. My father gave me discipline, an unshakable work ethic, and an example of what it meant to take your craft seriously. And Hollywood—well, Hollywood gave me a taste of the stage before I was even old enough to know what it meant to truly stand on one.

I didn't ask to be born into the spotlight. None of us kids do. But once the light finds you, it never really lets go.

Chapter 2

The Dreamer and the Rebel

Teenage years are supposed to be about figuring yourself out—testing boundaries, discovering passions, and carving out a future that feels like your own. For me, it was a time caught between two very different worlds: the dreamer who wanted to pitch under Friday night lights and the rebel who couldn't resist breaking every rule in the book.

Before Hollywood truly consumed me, my first love was baseball. I lived for the smell of the grass, the crack of the bat, the weight of a ball in my hand. Out on that diamond, it didn't matter who my dad was or what movies he had starred in. There were no scripts, no cameras—just the purity of the game. I dreamed of making it to the big leagues, wearing a uniform that had nothing to do with my last name. That dream gave me focus. It gave me a sense of identity that was mine and mine alone.

But alongside the dreamer in me lived a restless spirit—the rebel. The same intensity that made me a fierce competitor on the field also made me a kid who couldn't sit still. Malibu was paradise, but even paradise has shadows. The freedom of that world—the parties, the late nights, the crowd of friends who lived like rules didn't apply to them—was intoxicating. And I was never one to say no to a thrill.

I had friends who pushed boundaries the way surfers push waves. We cut class, chased girls, and looked for every opportunity to make the night last longer than it should. To us, trouble wasn't something to avoid; it was something to chase. We wore recklessness like a badge of honor. It made us feel invincible.

Still, Hollywood was always there, hovering in the background, reminding me that my life wasn't going to be typical no matter how hard I tried. Directors came by the house. Producers knew my name before I knew theirs. I'd watch my father's world up close and think, *Maybe I belong here too.* Acting wasn't just a family business—it was a gravitational pull. The idea of stepping into a role, of living someone else's life for a while, was thrilling.

But here's the thing: baseball and Hollywood weren't just two separate paths. They represented two parts of me. One side wanted structure, teamwork, the grind of practices and discipline. The other side craved freedom, excitement, and chaos. And as I got older, it became harder to balance those worlds.

When you're a teenager, you think you have time to do everything, to chase every dream and survive every mistake. I didn't know it then, but the wild streak that made me the life of the party would one day become the same fire that nearly consumed me. For now, though, I was just a kid with a fast pitch, a restless spirit, and the nagging feeling that Hollywood's call would be louder than any stadium cheer.

Looking back, I can see that those years were a rehearsal for the life I would eventually lead. Baseball taught me passion and precision. My friends taught me loyalty and recklessness in equal measure. And the lure of Hollywood—always shimmering on the horizon—taught me that destiny has a way of pulling you toward it, even if you're not ready.

I was a dreamer. I was a rebel. And together, those two sides of me were about to collide in ways I could never have imagined.

Chapter 3

Breaking Through: Hollywood Calling

When I finally made my way into Hollywood, it didn't feel like a single door opening—it felt like walking into a house I had been circling all my life. Acting wasn't new to me. I had been around sets since childhood, watching my father transform into other people with such conviction that I sometimes forgot he wasn't the character he was playing. But stepping into it myself, auditioning, learning to deliver lines, and carrying the weight of someone else's vision—that was a different kind of education.

My early gigs were small. Bit parts here and there, often overshadowed by the last name I carried. People were curious: *Can Martin Sheen's son act, or is he just cashing in on the family business?* That question hung in every audition room. I felt it every time I walked onto a set. The truth is, I had something to prove—not only to the industry but also to myself.

Then came *Platoon*. Oliver Stone was a force of nature, a director who wanted authenticity above all else. He didn't just want actors—he wanted soldiers. He threw us into a boot camp in the middle of the jungle, stripping away whatever Hollywood polish we carried with us. We lived like the men we were portraying: eating their food, sleeping in their mud, and carrying the same exhaustion and fear.

It was brutal, but it was real. And for me, it was transformative. *Platoon* wasn't just a movie—it was a baptism by fire. By the time the cameras rolled, I wasn't pretending to be a soldier. I *was* one. And when audiences saw it, they didn't see "Martin Sheen's kid." They saw a young actor willing to bleed for the story he was telling.

The success of *Platoon* opened doors I hadn't dared to dream about. Suddenly, I wasn't just in the room—I was being invited to sit at the table. And it wasn't long before another opportunity came knocking, one that would solidify my place in Hollywood: *Wall Street*.

Working alongside Michael Douglas and under Oliver Stone again, I found myself in the center of a story that cut to the bone of American ambition and greed. Playing Bud Fox wasn't just another role—it was a chance to show range, to embody the hunger of a young man who wanted everything, even if it cost him his soul.

The irony wasn't lost on me. Bud Fox's hunger mirrored my own. I wanted respect, recognition, success—and I was willing to throw myself into the fire to get it. But there was also a warning embedded in that story, a reflection of what can happen when desire turns into obsession. At the time, I didn't see it as a cautionary tale. I saw it as my arrival.

When *Wall Street* hit theaters, the industry took notice. People weren't just asking if I could act anymore—they were saying I *could*. Reviews called me promising, intense, even magnetic. For the first time in my life, the last name "Sheen" wasn't the headline. It was *Charlie* they were talking about.

Those years were a whirlwind. Red carpets, late-night interviews, scripts piling up on my desk. I was living the dream I had once only flirted with from the sidelines. But fame has a way of moving faster than you can prepare for. One minute you're chasing roles, the next minute the roles are chasing you—and with them comes everything else: the parties, the temptations, the sense that the rules don't apply anymore.

Breaking through in Hollywood felt like winning the lottery. But like most jackpots, it came with fine print I wasn't ready to read. All I knew then was that I had arrived. I was no longer just Martin Sheen's son. I was Charlie Sheen, and Hollywood was calling my name loud enough for the whole world to hear.

Chapter 4

Fame at Full Speed

Success doesn't tap you politely on the shoulder—it crashes into you like a wave. One moment, you're hustling for auditions, the next you're riding in limos, flying first class, and sitting at tables you once thought were reserved for legends. After *Platoon* and *Wall Street*, Hollywood didn't just know my name—they couldn't stop saying it.

The checks were bigger than I'd ever imagined. Overnight, I went from wondering if I'd book another role to wondering what I was supposed to do with all the money piling into my bank account. It wasn't just wealth—it was permission. Permission to buy, to travel, to indulge. Every door I knocked on flew open, and behind each one was another temptation waiting with a smile.

And here's the thing about fame: it doesn't just give you access. It rewrites the rules. People laugh at your jokes even if they're not funny. They forgive your mistakes before you've even said sorry. They want to be close to you—not because of who you are, but because of what you represent. The attention was addictive, the energy overwhelming. I was the center of a storm, and for a while, I loved every second of it.

The parties got bigger. The nights got longer. What started as champagne toasts after a premiere turned into after-hours marathons with drinks, drugs, and strangers who felt like best friends for the night. I told myself it was part of the lifestyle—that this was what success was supposed to look like. Work hard, play harder. And I played harder than anyone I knew.

My house in Malibu became a revolving door. Friends, hangers-on, people who wanted a taste of the wild ride—I welcomed them all. To me, it felt like freedom. No curfews, no limits, no boundaries. If there was a line to be crossed, I sprinted past it.

At the same time, my career kept soaring. Movies were coming one after the other, each one cementing my place as Hollywood's go-to for charm with an edge. I was on sets during the day, living characters with intensity, and by night, I was back to being Charlie—the guy who wanted the night to never end. It was a double life, except both sides were out in the open.

Of course, excess always carries a price tag. The late nights bled into early mornings. Hangovers turned into habits. What felt like control was already slipping away, though I didn't want to admit it. I told myself I could handle it. That I could keep riding the wave without being pulled under.

The truth? Fame was moving faster than I was. It felt like driving a Ferrari at full throttle down a twisting road. Exhilarating, yes. But one wrong turn, and everything could go up in flames.

At that time, though, I wasn't thinking about wrong turns. I was too busy chasing the rush. The applause, the flashing cameras, the whispered invitations to the next exclusive party—it was intoxicating. And I wasn't just sipping from the cup of success—I was drinking it dry.

Fame at full speed is a thrill like no other. But it's also a trap. And though I couldn't see it yet, the faster you go, the harder the crash waiting just around the corner.

Chapter 5

The Shadow of Addiction

At first, it all felt manageable. A drink here, a line there, a pill to keep the night going—Hollywood indulgence, nothing more. I told myself I wasn't doing anything different from half the people in the industry. Everyone partied. Everyone chased the high. Why should I be any different?

But addiction doesn't walk into your life and announce itself. It creeps in quietly, wearing the mask of fun, until one day you realize fun has turned into survival.

The nights got longer, the mornings harder. What used to be a celebration turned into a routine. Alcohol wasn't about raising a glass anymore—it was about steadying my hands, calming my nerves, numbing the pressure. Drugs weren't about curiosity or thrill—they were about control, or at least the illusion of it.

On set, I could still perform. Acting was my anchor, the one place where discipline still showed up. I'd throw myself into a role with everything I had, and for those hours, I could pretend nothing else was wrong. But once the cameras stopped rolling, the other Charlie took over—the restless, reckless one who always needed more.

My reputation began to shift. People whispered about my behavior, about my late arrivals and my wild nights. Directors started asking if I was reliable. Producers hesitated before calling. I was too caught up in the haze to notice that cracks were forming in the career I had fought so hard to build.

The truth was, I was chasing two highs at once—the high of applause and the high of escape. And the second one was winning.

Relationships suffered too. Friends who had been close began to drift, tired of the chaos that followed me everywhere. Romances turned volatile, fueled by late nights and bad decisions. Even my family, who loved me through everything, struggled to recognize the version of me who seemed determined to self-destruct.

The scariest part? I thought I was in control. I told myself I could stop anytime I wanted. That I was choosing the chaos, not the other way around. But the shadow of addiction had already wrapped itself around me, whispering lies I wanted to believe.

Looking back now, I can see how reckless I was, how blind I had become to the damage I was causing—not just to my career, but to myself. Addiction doesn't just take your health. It takes your time, your relationships, your sense of self. It strips away pieces of you until all that's left is the craving.

On the surface, I was still the Hollywood star, the guy audiences loved on screen. But behind the curtain, I was slipping fast. Fame had given me everything I thought I wanted. Addiction was about to show me how quickly it could all be taken away.

Chapter 6

Love, Lust, and Loss

Love has always been complicated for me. On screen, romance is scripted—it's neat, passionate, wrapped in a bow of happy endings. Off screen, real love is messy. Add fame, money, and addiction into the mix, and it becomes a storm that's almost impossible to steer.

I've never been short on romance. Women were drawn to the spotlight I carried, and I was drawn to them just as much. Sometimes it was lust, sometimes it was love, and sometimes it was just two lonely people trying to find a connection in a world that never slowed down. But I'll be the first to admit: I wasn't good at balance.

My relationships often started like a fire—intense, consuming, impossible to ignore. But like fire, they burned hot and fast, often leaving wreckage behind. Marriage was supposed to be different. It was supposed to be the anchor, the thing that gave me stability when the rest of my life was spinning out of control. And for a while, it was. I fell in love, got married, and welcomed children into my life—moments that still stand out as some of the most beautiful in all the chaos.

Becoming a father changed me in ways I didn't expect. Holding my kids for the first time, I felt a sense of responsibility I couldn't shrug off. They were pure, untouched by fame, addiction, or the mistakes I carried with me. In their eyes, I wasn't Charlie Sheen the actor—I was Dad. And that role mattered more than any movie or paycheck ever could.

But love and family require consistency, and consistency wasn't something I had. My addictions, my wild streak, my inability to separate the man from the myth—they all spilled into my relationships. Arguments turned explosive.

Promises were broken. Too many times, the people I loved most paid the price for the chaos I brought into their lives.

The public nature of my relationships didn't help. Every fight, every misstep, every headline became fodder for tabloids. My private heartbreaks were served up for the world's entertainment. Losing love is hard enough without cameras capturing your lowest moments.

And yet, I kept trying. I kept searching for that balance between the man who wanted to be a loyal partner and the man who couldn't let go of the spotlight or the lifestyle it offered. I wanted to be both, but too often I failed at both.

Still, through every marriage and breakup, through every headline about scandal or heartbreak, one constant remained: my love for my children. No matter how broken I was, no matter how reckless, the bond I shared with them kept me tethered to some version of myself that was still worth fighting for.

Love, lust, and loss—those three forces defined much of my personal life. They lifted me, broke me, and humbled me.

And though I didn't always handle them with grace, they reminded me of something I had almost forgotten in the chaos of fame: at the end of the day, what matters most are the people who stand by you when the cameras are gone and the lights have dimmed.

Chapter 7

Sitcom King: Winning at Prime Time

By the early 2000s, Charlie Sheen had lived through highs most people could only dream of, and lows most couldn't survive. Hollywood had seen him as the young, brooding star of *Platoon* and *Wall Street*, then as the troubled bad boy, tabloid headline fodder, and box-office gamble. But life had a strange way of circling back. Just when many thought his story was winding down, television handed him a second act—one that would not only redefine his career, but also etch his name into entertainment history.

It began when he replaced Michael J. Fox on *Spin City* in 2000. Stepping into someone else's shoes is never easy, but

Charlie's quick wit, sharp timing, and natural charisma made him a natural fit. The performance won him a Golden Globe and, more importantly, showed producers and networks that Sheen wasn't done yet. Far from it—he had just discovered the power of television.

That momentum carried him to *Two and a Half Men*. Premiering in 2003, the show was simple in concept: a carefree bachelor suddenly has to share his Malibu home with his uptight brother and young nephew. But what elevated it beyond formula was Charlie himself. Playing "Charlie Harper," a jingle-writing playboy who drank too much, slept around, and reveled in life's pleasures, was—let's be honest—just a stone's throw from Sheen's real persona. The line between character and actor blurred in a way that audiences found irresistible.

The chemistry on screen was lightning in a bottle. Jon Cryer's neurotic brother and Angus T. Jones's innocent, growing-up-too-fast nephew set the perfect stage for Sheen's larger-than-life charm. Week after week, the sitcom drew millions. Ratings soared, critics praised his effortless delivery, and suddenly Charlie Sheen wasn't just back—he was on top.

By 2010, *Two and a Half Men* was the most-watched comedy on television, and Sheen was the highest-paid actor in TV history, pulling in nearly $2 million per episode. Every Monday night, America tuned in to watch him wink, quip, and saunter through thirty minutes of laughter. He was no longer just a movie star who'd lost his way; he was television's king, commanding attention with every smirk.

But success at that level came with its own complications. The work schedule was demanding, the media spotlight was relentless, and behind the scenes, old habits still lurked. The irony wasn't lost on Charlie: he was being celebrated and rewarded for playing a version of himself—an unapologetic hedonist—while struggling to keep that same persona from swallowing his real life whole.

For the moment, though, the triumph outweighed the turbulence. He had rebuilt his image, secured generational wealth, and proved he could reinvent himself. Fans adored him, networks banked on him, and he had found a way to channel his excesses into art.

Charlie Sheen, the "bad boy of Hollywood," had officially become the king of prime time.

Chapter 8

Meltdown in the Spotlight

The crown Charlie Sheen wore as television's highest-paid star didn't slip quietly—it exploded in front of the entire world. What had begun as whispers about his hard partying and on-set clashes quickly spiraled into one of the most bizarre, unforgettable public breakdowns in pop culture history.

The signs had been there. His off-screen lifestyle mirrored his *Two and a Half Men* character too closely. The late-night benders, the erratic behavior, the wild parties—it all became harder to separate from his performance. When tensions boiled over with creator Chuck Lorre in 2011, it was more than just a workplace dispute; it was the spark that set off a firestorm.

Charlie didn't retreat quietly. Instead, he went on the offensive, granting interviews that seemed less like damage control and more like performance art. Sitting across from news anchors, he spoke in a rapid-fire stream of soundbites that would become memes overnight: "Tiger Blood," "Adonis DNA," "Winning." His words were outrageous, surreal, and at times nonsensical—but they were undeniably magnetic.

The media couldn't look away. Neither could the public. Clips of his rants went viral before "viral" had even cemented its place in the internet lexicon. Twitter feeds lit up with his quotes, late-night hosts turned him into punchlines, and suddenly Charlie wasn't just an actor in a sitcom—he was the center of a global spectacle.

But beneath the comedy and chaos was something darker. Fans and critics alike debated whether his behavior was a clever act of rebellion against Hollywood hypocrisy, or a man unraveling in real time. Some admired his defiance, others pitied his obvious struggles. Through it all, Charlie leaned into the storm, convinced he was untouchable.

The fallout was swift. Warner Bros. suspended production of *Two and a Half Men*. Lawsuits flew. Headlines dissected every move, every word, every public appearance. In less than a year, the king of prime time had lost his throne, his show, and, for many, his credibility.

And yet, the meltdown didn't erase him—it transformed him. Charlie Sheen had become something larger than his roles, larger even than his scandals. He was a cultural phenomenon, a living cautionary tale, and an internet legend all at once.

The world had seen stars crash and burn before, but rarely with such spectacle. For better or worse, Charlie Sheen wasn't just in the spotlight—he *was* the spotlight.

Chapter 9

Fallout and Reinvention

When the dust settled after Charlie Sheen's public meltdown, the empire he had built around *Two and a Half Men* was gone. The studio cut ties, his co-stars distanced themselves, and Ashton Kutcher stepped in to replace him. For a man who had once commanded nearly $2 million per episode, the fall was staggering. Overnight, Charlie went from being the most bankable sitcom star in America to a Hollywood outcast.

But if there's one thing Sheen had always known how to do, it was to reinvent himself.

The months that followed his firing were filled with lawsuits, negotiations, and the awkward silence of Hollywood executives unsure of what to do with him. Yet, Charlie refused to fade. He hit the road with his "Violent

Torpedo of Truth" tour, a chaotic mix of stand-up, storytelling, and sheer spectacle. The reviews were brutal at first—audiences didn't know what to make of it—but for Charlie, it was proof he could still draw a crowd. Even at his lowest, people wanted to see what he would do next.

That energy carried him to his next big gamble: *Anger Management*. In 2012, FX gave Charlie another shot, building a sitcom around him that loosely mirrored his public persona—a therapist with anger issues. It was a clever nod to his real-life struggles, and though critics weren't always kind, the show found an audience. At its peak, it drew millions of viewers, reminding the industry that Sheen's name still had weight.

This chapter of reinvention wasn't just about television, though. Charlie threw himself into side projects, from endorsements to social media experiments, where his offbeat humor and no-filter honesty attracted millions of followers. He leaned into the mythology of "Sheen the Survivor," a man who had lost it all but refused to disappear quietly.

Behind the scenes, though, the reinvention was fragile. Old habits lingered. Business relationships were strained. And while *Anger Management* offered redemption of sorts, it never reached the cultural heights of *Two and a Half Men*. It was, in many ways, the story of a man caught between past glory and future possibility.

Still, the very fact that Charlie managed to claw his way back onto TV at all was remarkable. In an industry quick to discard its fallen stars, he had once again bent the narrative in his favor.

Charlie Sheen may have lost his sitcom crown, but he proved something else in the aftermath: no matter how chaotic, no matter how messy, he had an uncanny ability to reinvent himself—and to keep the world watching.

Chapter 10

Facing the Truth

For most of his life, Charlie Sheen had lived in extremes—extreme fame, extreme indulgence, extreme chaos. But there came a point when the showmanship, the bravado, and the headlines couldn't cover the truth anymore. The masks he wore for Hollywood, for the media, and even for himself began to crack. What emerged was a man forced to face his demons, not as punchlines or catchphrases, but as life-or-death realities.

Addiction had been a constant shadow. For years, Charlie had shrugged it off with humor, cloaked it in defiance, or simply denied the depth of it. But behind closed doors, he was fighting battles that weren't glamorous or funny—days lost to drugs, relationships broken, health deteriorating. It wasn't just about being the Hollywood bad boy anymore; it was about survival.

Then came the most difficult revelation of all. In 2015, Charlie went public with his HIV diagnosis. The announcement shocked the world, but for him, it was a release of a secret that had weighed heavily for years. He spoke candidly about the fear, the stigma, and the shame that accompanied the diagnosis, but also about the strength he found in finally telling the truth. For perhaps the first time in decades, he wasn't performing—he was being real.

The confession was both devastating and liberating. It stripped away the last layers of invincibility he had clung to and forced him to confront his own vulnerability. Yet, it also opened the door to clarity. Facing the truth gave Charlie a chance to stop running from himself.

In interviews, he admitted his mistakes without the manic energy of his "Tiger Blood" era. He spoke with a quieter voice, one tinged with regret but also with a strange peace. The same man who once claimed to have "Adonis DNA" now admitted he was flawed, mortal, and still searching for balance.

There were still struggles—addiction doesn't vanish with a confession, and health battles don't resolve overnight. But there were also glimpses of resilience. Charlie committed to treatment, tried to repair relationships with his children, and even used his platform to raise awareness about living with HIV.

For a man who had spent decades as a caricature of excess, these moments of honesty revealed something the public hadn't always seen: Charlie Sheen, the human being.

Facing the truth didn't erase the past. It didn't undo the chaos or silence the critics. But it marked a turning point—a moment when, for once, Charlie stopped trying to win the spotlight and instead began trying to win himself back.

Chapter 11

Redemption and Recovery

Redemption doesn't come all at once. It isn't marked by a single moment, but by countless small choices—some triumphant, some painful, all requiring persistence. For Charlie Sheen, the road to recovery was less about erasing the past and more about learning how to live with it, to face it honestly, and to build something meaningful in its shadow.

Sobriety was the first step, though it was never simple. After years of cycles—relapse, denial, temporary clarity—Charlie had to embrace a truth that millions of others in recovery also face: it's not about perfection, but progress. He began to recognize his triggers, to seek help instead of hiding, and to surround himself with people willing to hold him accountable. There were stumbles along the way, but each stumble was followed by the decision to get back up. That in itself was a victory.

Just as important was repairing his role as a father. For too long, his children had seen the chaos of his public life overshadow the love he felt for them. Redemption meant showing up—not in grand gestures, but in the everyday acts of parenting: being present at a school event, listening without distraction, offering consistency where once there had been instability. The effort was ongoing, and imperfect, but it was real.

Family ties extended beyond his children, too. His relationship with his father, Martin Sheen, was complicated by years of worry and disappointment, yet grounded in an unshakable love. Martin had walked his own difficult path with addiction in his youth, and now he stood as both witness and guide to his son's attempt at renewal. Their bond, forged through pain and resilience, became a cornerstone of Charlie's healing.

Professionally, Charlie began to reframe his identity. No longer chasing the biggest paycheck or the wildest headlines, he leaned into quieter creative projects, ones that allowed him to connect rather than perform. He explored opportunities that reflected his lived experiences, whether through advocacy, writing, or mentorship. Slowly, he was redefining himself—not just as the star of *Platoon* or *Two and a Half Men*, but as a man who had survived, learned, and evolved.

Redemption didn't mean erasing the "Tiger Blood" years or denying the damage caused. Instead, it meant reclaiming ownership of his story. It meant recognizing that survival was not enough—he wanted to live with purpose, to be a better father, a better son, and ultimately, a better man.

Recovery, for Charlie Sheen, was not a finish line. It was, and remains, a journey. A daily choice to be honest, to stay present, and to believe that even after decades of chaos, healing is possible.

Chapter 12

Legacy of Laughter and Chaos

Few actors in Hollywood history have embodied both brilliance and bedlam quite like Charlie Sheen. His legacy is not a neat one—it is messy, unpredictable, and full of contradictions. Yet it is precisely that mix of laughter and chaos that has cemented him as a cultural icon, someone who will be remembered not only for the characters he played on screen, but also for the spectacle he created off it.

On the cinematic front, his performances in films like *Platoon* and *Wall Street* remain milestones of 1980s Hollywood. He was the handsome young star with sharp instincts, able to carry a film that would become part of America's cultural fabric. His early work proved that beneath the tabloid headlines and antics was genuine talent, a craft honed by discipline and natural charisma.

Then came television, where *Two and a Half Men* transformed him from a movie star with a fading reputation into the most-watched comedian on the planet. As Charlie Harper, Sheen delivered one-liners with effortless timing, making an entire generation laugh on Monday nights. For a while, he was America's favorite bad boy—and he was being paid accordingly.

But Charlie Sheen's cultural imprint goes far beyond traditional Hollywood. His infamous 2011 meltdown—complete with "Tiger Blood," "Adonis DNA," and the now-legendary declaration of "Winning!"—turned him into one of the internet's first true meme kings. His interviews were clipped, remixed, and shared endlessly online, making him both a laughingstock and a cult hero. In the digital age, Charlie Sheen was everywhere, shaping not just entertainment but internet humor itself.

For some, his legacy is a cautionary tale: the dangers of fame, addiction, and excess played out for the world to see. For others, he represents defiance—the man who broke the rules, mocked authority, and refused to bow to Hollywood's expectations. And for many, he is both: a reminder that genius and self-destruction can live side by side, often in the same person.

What is undeniable is that Charlie Sheen left a mark. His name still sparks recognition, his quotes still circulate, and his performances continue to entertain. He is proof that legacies don't always come wrapped in perfection; sometimes, they come wrapped in contradictions, chaos, and flashes of brilliance that refuse to fade.

Charlie Sheen's story may never fit into a clean narrative, but perhaps that is the point. His legacy is not about control—it's about impact. And love him or loathe him, the laughter he created and the chaos he embodied will forever be part of the cultural conversation.

Chapter 13

A New Chapter: Life After the Headlines

For decades, Charlie Sheen's life unfolded like a movie no scriptwriter could have dreamed up—complete with blockbuster highs, tragic lows, and scenes so outrageous they blurred the line between fact and fiction. But what happens when the cameras stop flashing, the headlines fade, and the noise of the world finally quiets down? For Charlie, it has meant stepping into a new chapter, one built not on spectacle but on something simpler: reflection.

Fame had given him everything—money, status, adoration—but it had also taken its toll. In quieter moments, Charlie has admitted that the spotlight can be both a blessing and a curse. The fame amplified his triumphs, but it also magnified his mistakes. Every stumble, every misstep, every failure was broadcast to the world, immortalized in tabloids and on the internet. It is a weight few can understand, and one he carried for years with a mix of bravado and denial.

Now, though, he sees it differently. With distance comes perspective, and with perspective comes forgiveness—both of others and of himself. He does not deny the wreckage left behind by addiction, ego, and reckless choices. Instead, he owns it. But in owning it, he also claims the right to move forward, to define himself by more than his worst chapters.

Fatherhood has become one of the most important anchors in this process. For all his fame and notoriety, Charlie often says his greatest role has been that of a father. His children have seen him at his most vulnerable and his most resilient, and rebuilding those relationships has been central to his redemption. Being present, being honest, and being steady—these are the things that matter most to him now, more than ratings or record-breaking paychecks ever could.

And so, what does Charlie Sheen want his story to stand for? Not just the chaos, though he knows that will always be part of the legend. Not just the laughter, though he's grateful for every smile he's brought to an audience. What he hopes, above all, is that people see the resilience—the ability to fall, to fail spectacularly, and yet still find a way to get back up. He wants his story to remind others that it's never too late to change, to repair, to redefine yourself.

Life after the headlines is quieter, yes, but it is also richer in ways fame never provided. For Charlie Sheen, the new chapter is not about chasing "winning." It's about peace, forgiveness, love, and the simple act of being present in a world that once spun out of control.

Made in United States
North Haven, CT
12 September 2025